AF265380

killing me
from the inside
out

remy nash

to the warriors

we take one step ahead

without stumbling

contents

killing me

from the inside

out

death

remy nash

painkiller overdose.
sleeping meds with rum.
correction fluid ingestion.
partial suspension hanging.
cutting.
endless hours of starvation.
nightly pleas to the universe.

so many attempts at death.
though still i live.

i wonder at times
if there was ever a point.

until i remember:

i was trying to kill myself
before she could do it herself.

a demon from
the realm beyond,
one with charm,
she tricked others all
too well.

disguised as a saint,
telling lies
to lead followers
high and above,
she carried all
down below
to burn in the fire
where she dwelled.

from the surface

grew her petals and leaves,

concealing the thorns

she aspired to

keep unseen.

engraved on my skin,
the scars of lost battles.

each with its own story
of me being defeated
at every war i fought.

against myself.

— *self-inflicted wounds*

frozen like rime,

bitter and gelid

like the ice

forming my empty chest.

cold.

numb.

meaningless.

— i felt, i was

enclosed in a glass cage,

watching outward

as time passed and passed.

a spectre without a worry

taunted me from the other side.

how callous it was,

to be so cruel and wicked.

how awful it was,

to be so malicious and spiteful.

a spectre without a worry

taunted me from the other side.

enclosed in a glass cage,

i watched

as time passed and passed.

— *the malignant spirit*

never could i

do right.

only wrong.

— *always losing*

staring at the off-white walls
in my prison,
watching the seasons come and go.

for years.

when the flowers emerged,
i remained hidden.

while the sun beamed brightly,
i remained hidden.

as leaves fell from the lush trees,
i remained hidden.

when snow and ice wrecked havoc,
i flourished.

the only parts left of me,

whenever around her,

were different forms of misery.

— *broken into fragments*

when darkness reigned,
i felt my best.

i relished the shadows.

it was in the night
where i sat on my throne,
when all were asleep,
for no one attempted
to overthrow my ruling.

— *midnight royalty*

her love was parasitic,

sucking away my energy,

quickly draining

my desire to live,

my drive to continue.

— *tainted love*

i could hardly breathe.

ever.

every morning

that i was awake,

my body was numb,

my soul was cast to sleep.

— eternal slumber

rip out the pounding heart
from within my chest
so i can no longer feel.

cut every muscle in my body
into pieces too small to define
so i can no longer be strong.

take control over my mind
so i can no longer think
for myself.

turn me into exactly who
you want me to be.

it was your mission anyway.

i felt nothing

but emptiness.

always.

the plants around me
withered a little more
each day.

once upon a time,
they told brilliant stories.
until they began
ignoring me,
speaking less and less
as the months went on,
slowly dying
just to escape.

the trees were becoming bare.

leaves fell slowly to the ground.

a faint wind passed,
drifting them metres away
from where they were
meant to land.

and there they dried up.

until meeting their doom.

— *without sustenance*

no longer did my shadow

follow from behind.

it surrounded me

like darkness

suffocating the light.

i never spoke words.

the gloom on my face

told all the stories

needed.

— *storytelling*

and everyone wondered

where the gleam in my eyes

had gone.

she wanted to lock me

in her world of treachery,

for i was never expected

to thrive when with her.

a world of emptiness

was where i belonged,

down under,

to a place

no one wandered.

a portrait existed,

one of me,

unique and delicate,

special and exquisite.

it was cursed,

meant to change

by how my soul evolved

while my body remained fair

like an illusion to curious eyes.

the portrait,

it was once picturesque.

but now grotesque.

— the picture of ...

she was an emissary

of the afterlife,

eager to collect lives,

hungry to feed.

the deceptive beast hid within

a beautiful young woman,

desperate to lure fools

to meet their end.

i was the prey,

blinded and manipulated,

naive and trusting.

— *tricked*

i was always in mourning,

watching myself meet

a steady and gloomy death.

i was parched with heat.

i was burned to nothing.

dispersed along the ground,
i was meant to be walked on
as dirt beneath one's feet.

— *scatter into ashes*

the undead from below

rise at the darkest hour in the night

to claim another innocent

for company.

— *the forgotten*

the grim reaper wanted

to make me her servant.

she had plans for me.

33

rebirth

remy nash

the clock chimed at midnight.

i placed the crown atop
my head where it belonged
and marked my power.

i was a royal in the night.

and i knew then that
it would be the last time
i was made to feel differently.

— *midnight royalty ii*

a speck of light danced

from high above,

illuminating,

expanding until it was

large enough to consume.

the light was healing.

effortlessly purifying.

a feather fell from his back.

and then another.

— growing wings

the fire burned incredibly.

throughout the night.

until the sunny morning.

as bright as the sun.

just as scorching hot.

it was formidable
with a message quite telling:

the fire was meant to survive.

the flames ignited

to burn another day.

from beneath the ashes

left behind,

a creature was reborn.

— phoenix rising

the grey clouds

slowly drifted away.

from beyond the walls

that kept me held,

blue skies extended

as lucid as a dream.

— *revolution*

he had often felt fated
to idle the pathways alone,
wondering for how long
he would feel broken.

who have i become?
he wondered solemnly.
no longer am i myself.

how foolish the demon was

to think that deception

could last an eternity.

those days were numbered.

her time was limited.

the dark ones craving power

were fated to turn into dust.

a single tear

slid down his face.

yet he knew that

it was going to be

the last of its kind.

— *big boys never cry*

the mirror slid
through his fingers.

it fell to the ground,
shattering in pieces,
hundreds and hundreds
among many.

he stared at each fragment,
split and damaged,
unlike its original form.

he looked at the shards
scattered on the hardwood floor
and saw himself.

— *flawed reflection*

for the last time,

these wounds would

be scratched.

not a bone in his body

was broken,

yet he was recovering

from an injury,

which, at times,

left him unable to move.

a memory of who

i once aspired to be

flashed in my mind.

i then desired

to become the old me.

only greater.

when the light emerged,

he realized he was not

the person he thought

he was.

grow from the soil

of the earth,

even in the cruelest weather.

blossom until

the last of your days,

when you are unable to

no longer.

— *living*

there was a fire

within his soul

that helped him

take another leap,

farther and farther,

every evening.

i was crazy enough
to believe that i could
thrive.

yet i did.

dark clouds

no longer block my sight.

being lost

is a wonderful location

to discover who you are.

— discovery

long and daunting nights
have suddenly become
much shorter.

— *zzz*

he once dreamed

of happiness.

until it became

a reality.

he has shed

a hundred skins

to evolve into

the man he is today.

feeling so good.

about the book

killing me from the inside out is a collection of short poetry written by writer remy nash. the first part, *death*, deals with pain, heartbreak, abuse; the second part, *rebirth*, deals with change, self-worth, finding happiness.

www.ingramcontent.com/pod-product-compliance
Lightning Source LLC
Chambersburg PA
CBHW051007050726
47592CB00007B/2745